America's
BALD EAGLE

America's
BALD EAGLE

WRITTEN AND PHOTOGRAPHED BY

HOPE RYDEN

G. P. PUTNAM'S SONS
New York

J
598.9
R

48840

Copyright © 1985 by Hope Ryden
All rights reserved. Published simultaneously in
Canada by General Publishing Co. Limited, Toronto.
Printed in the United States of America
First Impression
Design by Nanette Stevenson

Library of Congress Cataloging in Publication Data
Ryden, Hope.
America's bald eagle.
Includes index.
1. Bald eagle—Juvenile literature.   I. Title.
QL696.F32R93   1985   598'.916   84-18234
ISBN 0-399-21181-0

ACKNOWLEDGMENTS

I wish to thank U.S. Forest Service wildlife biologist John Mathisen for directing me to viewable eagle eyries in the Chippewa National Forest in Minnesota, where I was able to observe and photograph eagle nesting behavior. I am even more grateful to him for his ideas on nest protection, which have been implemented by the U.S. Forest Service. For information gained during discussions with Dr. Tom Dunstan of Western Illinois University, professor Dan Frenzel of the University of Minnesota, biologist Janet Moline of Rock Island, Illinois and filmmaker Herman Kitchen, I am also indebted. For their participation in the shooting of pictures on pages 37 and 38, I wish to thank biologists Jay Tobin and Norman Weiland, who invited me to observe them tagging nestlings and whose climbing skills are something to marvel about. Pictures on pages 28 and 31 are courtesy of the U.S. Forest Service. I hardly know how to express my admiration for professor Gary Duke and Dr. Patrick Redig, cofounders of the Raptor Research and Rehabilitation Center at the University of Minnesota, where scores of injured eagles have been repaired and returned to the wild. These two men generously shared their knowledge and insights with me. I also owe a special thanks to biologist Julie Lee for arranging photographic opportunities for me at the Carpenter St. Croix Valley Nature Center in Hastings, Minnnesota. Pilot Mark Shough deserves my salute for his skillful maneuvering of a Cessna 172 during an eight-hour survey of nesting eagles in the Chippewa National Forest. I shall never forget the experience! And to Bob and Jane Smith, who lent me the use of their North Twin Lake cabin, and to Jack Penn, who lent me his boat, my thanks. I am also appreciative of the help from Ashley "Buzz" Benjamin who directed me to an excellent eagle wintering area in New York state, which location he would prefer I not publicize.

Finally, I am grateful for the comments of Roger Tory Peterson who read this manuscript prior to publication.

H. R.

Hope Ryden's new book tells us much that we should know about the bald eagle, our national symbol. These days eagles are receiving a great deal of attention. Each fall groups of people gather at such lookouts as Hawk Mountain in Pennsylvania to observe bald eagles as they fly down the ridges. In Glacier National Park in Montana and at dams along the Mississippi River hundreds of eagle watchers also await the arrival of these majestic birds, which are attracted by dead and stranded fish. At Klamath Falls in Oregon, perhaps as many as 600 bald eagles spend the winter. One morning before breakfast I counted more than 190 as they flew from their roost. The Chilkat in southeastern Alaska is seasonal host to several thousand of these birds, which come from all parts of that large state to take advantage of the salmon run.

Another facet of the eagles' world which Hope Ryden writes about is "hacking," the introduction of captive eagles into the wild. This type of restoration program is being carried out successfully in several states where breeding eagles had become almost nonexistent.

In addition she tells about raptor rehabilitators, those humanitarian people who take care of eagles that have been injured or shot.

Her splendidly detailed account of the bird's habits clearly demonstrates that America's national symbol is a multifaceted bird. It fascinates not only a growing army of bird watchers, but also nature lovers of every taste.

Hope Ryden's book is a salute to this glorious bird.

Roger Tory Peterson

The North American bald eagle is a creature of high places. It floats and spirals in air space high above the earth. Sometimes it flies so high it cannot be seen from the ground. When it comes to rest, it alights on the topmost branches of tall trees, lookouts from which it can scan the countryside. Only to pick up food does it descend to the earth's surface, skimming along a lake or river in swift pursuit of a fish or dipping into an open field to snag a small mammal with its sharp talons. It soon rises. The bald eagle is not at home on the ground, for unlike chickens or grouse or pheasants, whose feet are designed for walking, the eagle's curved talons make ground travel awkward. Nor are its wings made for low altitude flight through dense stands of trees. When spread, they measure seven feet or more across. So the bald eagle spends its time in the high places and seeks a lofty cradle in which to rear its young, a towering tree whose crown rises above the surrounding forest canopy. There, eighty to one hundred feet above the ground, it lays its eggs. There its chicks hatch high and early learn that they, too, are destined to be sky dwellers.

Even though few people today have seen a North American bald eagle, just about everybody knows what one looks like. It is our national bird. Its likeness decorates many government buildings and, during election campaigns, its image is often flashed on television. Turn a quarter or a silver dollar to the tail side and you will see this bird. The bald eagle stands for the United States of America. It was the symbol chosen by our founding fathers to appear on our country's seal. A country's seal is a kind of signature. Just as a person must sign his name to important papers to make them legal, so a government must stamp its documents with its own special seal to make them official.

Great Seal of the United States

A bald eagle under the age of five looks entirely different from one that has lived five years or longer. Eagles under five are large, dark birds with brown eyes and dark beaks. Eagles five years and older wear white hoods over their heads (which, by the way are not bald), sport flashy white tails and peer at the world through yellow eyes. Their beaks, too, are yellow.

All this can be baffling to bird-watchers who often mistake young bald eagles for vultures or for golden eagles (an entirely different species that nests mainly in the West). To make matters more confusing, young bald eagles change from one year to the next.

13

When first out of the nest, a young bald eagle is as glossy black as a raven's wing and, amazingly, it is larger than its own parents! By its second year of life, it has developed a smattering of light feathers across its breast, beneath its wing linings and under the base of its tail. It is irregularly marked, however, and looks like a bird in the process of *moulting*, or shedding old feathers for new ones.

During the next two or three years this mottled pattern persists. The bird remains basically dark but for small patches of lighter feathers. Then at age five the North American bald eagle changes dramatically. The bodies of male and female alike turn solid brown. Their dark eyes and beaks change to sunny yellow and their heads and tails become as gleaming white as a summer cloud. (Long ago, bald headed meant white headed.)

One can imagine the confusion that this has caused. Even the great naturalist, John James Audubon, was fooled by the bird. When our nation was young, Audubon traveled throughout North America, painting and describing all the birds he saw. In 1814, while floating down the Mississippi River, he noticed several dark eagles among a

14

flock of white-headed ones. Audubon did not suspect that these dark eagles were actually one-and-the-same species he knew well and had often painted. Believing he had discovered a new bird, he became very excited and he named it "Washington's Eagle," after George Washington, whom he greatly admired.

"If America has reason to be proud of her Washington," he wrote in his diary, "so has she to be proud of her eagle."

Audubon never learned of his mistake. Even after his death many people believed that three species of eagle inhabited North America.

In actual fact, North America is home to two species of eagle: the American bald eagle, whose scientific name is *Haliaeëtus leucocephalus* (Latin for white-headed eagle) and the golden eagle, whose scientific name is *Aquila chrysaëtos* (*chrysaëtos* means golden in Greek). Of these two birds, only the North American bald eagle can truly be called a native son, for it is found nowhere else but on our continent. Although the golden eagle lives and breeds here, it is also an inhabitant of northern Europe, Asia, the Middle East and North Africa.

Golden eagle

It is easy to confuse a golden eagle with a young bald eagle who has not yet put on its white headdress and tail. Given a close-up look at a golden eagle, however, one can see that its head has a metallic cast, as if it had been lightly sprayed with bronze paint. Also, its legs differ from those of the young bald eagle: They are feathered to the toes. Young bald eagles expose the lower third of their yellow "legs" and look as if they had hiked up their feathered trousers to go wading. (What appears to be a bird's "leg" is actually its foot.)

But these features are not easily spotted on birds that like to soar at altitudes of 1,000 feet and even higher. Perhaps a better way to distinguish one species from the other is to observe the birds' habits. A golden eagle feeds mostly on small ground animals, such as rabbits and gophers. One is apt to see it dive from the sky into a farmer's field or swoop down on a mountain meadow where such prey abound. Bald eagles, on the other hand, are mainly fisher birds. They are more likely to be seen gliding over rivers or making slow circles above lakes in search of easy targets.

Of course, on occasion, a bald eagle will hunt those small land animals favored by the golden eagle. Being a *predator*, or meat-eater, it cannot afford to pass up any food source. And being a predator, it has evolved the weapons it needs to obtain food. An eagle kills with its feet, driving its sharp curved talons deep to reach vital organs. When it seizes prey, certain muscles used to control grip lock in place. No matter how violently its victim may struggle to get free, an eagle cannot let go before these locked muscles relax.

An eagle is also armed with a hooked beak, which can do much damage. But this is seldom used to kill prey. An eagle's beak serves other purposes. With it, the bird tears its food into bite-sized pieces and passes morsels to its young. Even when defending itself, an eagle

18

rarely uses its beak. It prefers to ride back on its tail and strike with its sharp, grappling-hook talons, all the while hissing like a snake. Eagle researchers, who on occasion climb into nests to attach bands to the legs of young birds must be alert and stay clear of an eagle's talons. Anyone who is hooked by them has great difficulty prying the bird's locked claws loose. Even newly-hatched eagle chicks know how to make use of their feet in self-defense and strike at nest intruders.

Nature has equipped this high-flying hunting bird with still another useful feature—telescopic vision. Eagles are able to spy prey from great distances. Some experts have figured out that an eagle's eyesight is eight times better than man's. Moreover, an eagle's eye has two *foveae*, or centers of focus, allowing it to see both forward and sideways. It is easy to see how the expression "eagle-eyed" came into use. An eagle in flight can track a tiny mouse scurrying about on the ground!

It is fortunate for the eagle that it is so well designed for the hunt, for the life of a predatory bird is difficult at best. Compared to ground-dwelling birds, such as grouse or pheasants who feed on what seeds and grain lie at their feet, a predatory bird must work hard for its living. Because it lacks a gizzard, it is not able to digest vegetation and must catch and kill everything it eats. To do this requires both skill and superb health. A bald eagle must be superalert to spot prey. It must be superfast to overtake and capture prey. And it must be superpowerful to kill prey. An individual that lacks any of these physical attributes will not long survive.

Predatory birds are also called *raptors*. The raptor class includes eagles, owls, hawks, vultures and kites. Many people are not aware of the hardships faced by these meat-eaters. Some people are even under the impression that raptors are a menace to the prey species they feed upon. As a result, untold numbers of eagles, hawks and owls are shot from the sky by individuals who believe they are doing nature a favor. Nothing could be further from the truth.

Because prey species, such as rabbits and pheasants, have over long

Young great horned owl

Turkey vulture

Red-shouldered hawk

ages served as food for predatory birds and animals, they have evolved a high birthrate and thus quickly replace their losses. These species need no help from man to survive. By contrast, eagles and other hunters, having never served as food for other creatures, have evolved a low birthrate to hold them in balance with their food supply. When man preys on these hunters, he does much harm, for they are not able to make up for losses by producing more offspring.

It should come as no surprise, therefore, to learn that our national bird is not thriving. In forty-eight states, it is listed as threatened or endangered by the United States government. It never existed in Hawaii. Only in Alaska is the bird holding its own.

It is not for lack of trying that the bald eagle raises few young. No bird can be said to be a more attentive parent. Few species feed their helpless young over such a long period of time. Whereas the offspring of a robin or a wren are ready to leave their nest two weeks after hatching, bald eagle chicks require three months of parental care before they *fledge,* or launch themselves from their tree home.

This puts their parents on a tight schedule. There is, in fact, no room in the eagle's timetable for delays of any kind. Eagle eggs must be *incubated*, or sat upon, for thirty-five days before they hatch. Then eagle chicks do not become flightworthy for another twelve weeks. By the time the young leave their nest it is midsummer. This allows the young eagles only a few weeks to practice flying and fishing before lakes and rivers begin to freeze up. In the northern states, if a pair of eagles has not readied their big stick nest to receive eggs by early April at the latest, their young will fledge too late to learn all they need to know before they must head south for winter.

So northern eagles return to their breeding territories when snow is still on the ground. Immediately, they set about repairing and remodeling their nests of the previous year. Each year as much as a foot of sticks may be added to the huge structures. Over many years' time, an eagle's nest may grow so large that it topples the tree that holds it. Some eagle nests have been found that are as large as automobiles and weigh two thousand pounds.

22

Today so many forests have been cut that eagles have difficulty finding suitable places in which to build. A bald eagle nest must be situated in the uppermost branches of a very tall tree, one that rises above the surrounding forest. This is important because the big birds need plenty of clearance to make safe landings and takeoffs. The crown of the tree must be strong and properly formed to support a heavy nest. And it must contain bare branches that can be used for perching. Within line of sight, two or three additional lofty trees must rise out of the forest canopy. These will serve the parent birds as lookout posts. They will also be used as landing platforms by the young *eaglets* when they make their first gliding flight. Finally, the nest tree must grow near water. Although eagles do sometimes feed on small mammals and birds, ninety percent of what they eat is fish.

To obtain material to construct such a giant nest, or *eyrie*, requires much effort on the part of the birds. Sticks as big and round as a man's arm are needed. Since these cannot always be found lying about on the ground, the birds acquire them by flying at trees and snapping off dead limbs with their strong feet.

When an eyrie has been completed to a pair's satisfaction, it is scooped out and lined with grass, which the birds rake from a nearby meadow with their sharp talons. Then most eagle pairs do something strange. One of the birds breaks off a live branch of pine and jams the bough into the side of the nest. No one has been able to come up with an explanation for this behavior. Perhaps eagles like a touch of greenery in their brown stick home!

Should a pair of eagles discover, upon returning to their private breeding territory in early spring, that their nest tree has blown down or that their eyrie of the previous year has been torn apart by vandals or has been taken over by a pair of great horned owls who fiercely defend it, chances are the two will spend the entire breeding season rebuilding and will raise no young. But some eagle pairs have prepared for such calamities. These birds have built back-up nests— sometimes as many as four! Over many years time these extra eyries may stand empty. But when lightning, wind, tree rot, vandals or owl squatters put the pair out of their preferred nest, they waste no time settling into one of these standby structures. Eagles that are addicted to nest building are not so likely to lose a year of breeding time as are eagles that provide themselves but a single basket to hold their precious eggs.

If eagles do not always pair for life, most do stay with a chosen mate for many years. If either should die, the remaining bird quickly seeks a new partner. Otherwise, the two return to their customary nesting territory each spring; the first to arrive waits, watches, and even calls for the other.

Eagle courtship is a spectacle to behold. Doing a kind of sky dance, the two birds soar and wheel, dip and climb, come together and glance apart. They choose a windy day to perform their aerial acrobatics, a day when flying is easy. Strong currents of warm air, or *thermals*, carry them upwards to a great height, then treat them to long, free-coasting rides. Effortlessly, the birds float about the sky. By merely tilting a wing, they can change direction, bank or catch an air

current that lifts them yet higher. Again and again, a courting pair swoop at one another, then glide apart. Then, as if on signal, they make contact. In midair, one rolls under the other and reaches up to clasp its outstretched claws. Flying in this strange manner, the pair lose altitude. To slow their tumbling fall, they beat their wings rhythmically. At one moment the male finds himself beneath the female. Then the female cartwheels under him. As the ground speeds toward them, the birds separate, flapping vigorously to fight the pull of gravity. Then, caught by a thermal, they allow themselves to be carried skyward again.

These sky dances are a prelude to actual mating, which does not take place until the nest has been completed. Shortly afterward, the female lays a *clutch* of eggs, usually one or two. On rare occasions she may produce three.

Now the birds have no more leisure time to cruise about the sky together. One or the other must remain at the nest to keep the eggs warm. Although the somewhat larger female does most of the *incubating*, from time to time her mate relieves her. Should either bird grow restless and depart before the return of the other, the clutch is not left unprotected. Before taking off, the bird will bury the precious eggs under the grassy lining of the nest.

Not only must mated eagles protect the contents of their eyrie from owls and crows, they must also patrol their territory to prevent any other eagle couple from trying to occupy it. The mere sight of a strange eagle in what they consider to be their air space is certain to provoke them to throw back their heads and *chitter*. And should this cascade of strident cries fail to send the trespasser packing, one or the other will rise from its perch and, with talons extended, launch an all-out attack. Usually the aerial fight does not last long. Each bird

attempts to gain altitude on the other and dive at it. But the intruder soon withdraws. It has less at stake than does the nesting bird, and so it fights with less fervor.

When the time comes for an eagle chick to hatch, the parent birds can give it no help. The eaglet must work its own way out of its egg prison. Fortunately, nature has equipped it with an *egg tooth*—a tiny rhinoceros-type horn—on its upper beak. With this tool, which disappears shortly after birth, the chick pips tiny holes in the shell wall.

Al Grew

This is no easy task for it to accomplish. The imprisoned infant frequently grows tired from the effort and must take many rests. If all goes well, however, after some four hours' work, a half-circle of puncture holes will have been made. This weakened section of shell can then be easily punched out, and the chick is born.

A female eagle, as a rule, lays two eggs, although not on the same day. The first to be deposited, of course, is the first to hatch. Normally, the second chick does not break out of its shell until the first one is several days old. Given such a headstart, the first-born remains larger and stronger than its brother or sister throughout nest life. It normally is the first to fledge.

At one time it was widely believed that this older, larger eaglet routinely killed its nestmate in battles over food. But such deadly combat, if it ever occurs, must be rare. Although nestlings become highly excited when a fish is delivered and do get into squabbles, mealtime does not turn into a free-for-all. During most of nest life, a parent bird presides over whatever offering of mullet or shad or carp it has brought to the nest, tearing off bite-sized pieces which it then passes to each chick. Should an especially large portion be given either one, that chick will drag its prize to a far corner of the nest

where, with quivering wings, it will shriek loud warnings at its nest-mate to keep its distance.

Much later, when the young are about ready to leave the nest, the parents no longer beak-feed them. By then the eaglets are as large or larger than the adults, and, to avoid being mobbed by their unruly offspring, the parents often do not land on the eyrie when making a food delivery. Instead they fly over the nest and bomb the squealing nestlings with their catch. Whichever eaglet succeeds in taking possession of the food drop immediately covers it with outspread wings and, flapping and shrieking, keeps its nestmate at bay. After eating its fill, however, the triumphant eaglet loses interest in protecting its booty, and the bested chick is allowed a turn at it.

A newly hatched chick cannot walk. Until it is five weeks old it cannot even stand up. Nevertheless, a one-day-old chick will waddle about its huge nest on its shanks, using its stubby wings as crutches.

Jack Stuart

Al Grew

Some species of birds are born naked, but not the bald eagle. It breaks out into the world fully clothed in a coat of pale gray down. Its head and underparts are pure white. And its eyes and beak are beetle-black. This charming costume is soon shed for another. The bald eagle's habit of making itself over is already evident when it is a nestling. Eagle chicks wear three changes of dress even before they fledge.

After three weeks their first down is gone, replaced not by feathers but by a second coat of fuzz. This down is thick and wooly and darker than the first. By now the chicks have grown considerably and lost much of their infant appeal. In their second dress, one might even describe them as "ugly ducklings."

The parent birds, of course, take no notice of these changes in their offspring. As long as their young wear down of any description, the adults continue to *brood* them; one parent or the other tucks the chicks under its warm breast at night or when the weather is bad. Even after the eaglets have begun to grow feathers, the female bird shelters them under her arched, or *mantled*, wings whenever it storms or is windy.

31

Although the female of the pair is the more attentive parent, her mate is not "sexist" about what duties he performs. Both birds take turns baby-sitting and catering fish. While one hunts, the other remains on guard at the nest or watches for owls or ravens from a nearby *sentry tree*. Should any such nest robber approach, it is promptly chased.

So much is demanded of eagle parents, it is clear why they do not breed until age five. By then they are experienced fishers, able to satisfy their own hunger and deliver some four fish a day to a pair of chicks. Most human fishermen, equipped with fancy lures and tackle, would find this an impossible order to fill. Yet eagle parents, using only their own eyes and talons, manage to provide for their young day-in-and-day-out over a three-month period.

That they can even see fish swimming in the water from altitudes of several hundred feet is cause enough for amazement. To strike these veiled targets, they must then dive at speeds of seventy feet per second. Plummeting waterward, their feet drop like landing gears. Then, as they skim across the water, their claws sweep backward, feeling for a slippery form.

Most fish get away. Again and again eagles splash down and then climb skyward empty-footed. Little wonder they look for targets that have little or no play left in them. Perhaps half of what they catch is sick or dying. For when their tong-like talons do sink into the body of a lively pike or bullhead, what follows is a kind of death struggle between the sky-dwelling eagle and its victim, a creature of the deep. Neither animal wants to be pulled from its natural element. The fish, locked in the eagle's grip, tries to dive for the bottom. The eagle, unable to let go and flapping wildly to stay afloat, tries to rise.

Even when the fish begins to tire, success is by no means certain for the eagle. Without solid surface to push against and weighted down by its prize, the bird sometimes has difficulty achieving lift-off. Beating its wings laboriously, it must scoot across the surface of the water until it builds up speed for takeoff. After it gains a little altitude,

however, air currents buoy it higher and help it carry home its prize.

The young hear it coming and face the direction from which it approaches. As it nears the eyrie it calls and the chicks immediately assume their begging postures. Wings quivering, beaks thrust upward, they peep piteously.

Now the eagle must land its catch on the nest and make a one-

footed touchdown at the same time. One set of talons releases its tight clutch of the fish and reaches for a nest perch. Ballooning wings break the impact of landing. Dinner is delivered.

At five weeks of age the young eaglets can get up off their *tarsi* (Latin for foot bones) and walk on their toes like proper birds. Still, they waddle, parrot fashion. Their two-inch curved talons do not give

them good support. Several times a day they make their way to the edge of the eyrie, where they turn around and, balancing unsteadily, relieve themselves over the side. Eagle chicks do not foul their nests. As a result, a white chalky ring builds up around the base of their nest trees. This *guano* is excellent fertilizer and likely feeds the aging trees that eagles must have to support their huge eyries.

By this time the eaglets have begun to sprout feather tubes along their wings and tail. After a week these dangling pipes burst at one end to reveal a tip of black feather. Even this development, however, does little to improve the chicks' appearance. They now look like pin cushions stuck with dozens of fancy, feather-tipped hatpins.

Tobin/Ryden

As feathers grow in, the nestlings look more and more bedraggled—their bodies a patchwork of loose gray down and new black plumage. As if aware of their sorry appearance, they spend hours of every day *preening* themselves—arranging feathers and removing the loose fluff that hangs from their breasts and backs. Down floats about the eyrie like milkweed floss, and sparrows and titmice make daring raids to obtain it. By mid-June most songbirds are preparing to raise their second family of the season and they need soft material to reline their nests. Still, the young of the bald eagle are flightless.

By their eighth week of life, the young eaglets' third costume change is completed. Fully feathered and down-free at last, they look as black and sleek as a man's top hat. On their feet and legs they sport yellow boots. Their eyes have turned hazel. They bear not the slightest resemblance either to their former or to their future selves. That their parents even recognize these creatures as their own is

Weiland/Ryden

something of a wonder. It is fortunate they do. For yet another month the young eagles will remain nestbound.

Whether or not a pair of juvenile eagles, who by now have been confined to their high home for two months, can be said to experience boredom, there is no denying they begin to show signs of restlessness. Seeking playful outlet, they pull sticks from their eyrie and toss them high in the air. On occasion, the two may grab onto the same stick and prance about the nest with it, like a pair of dogs playing tug-of-war. Frequently, they tilt their heads sideways and eye the sky, watching for the return of a parent.

By now the adults have begun to relax their vigilance somewhat. Whichever one is on guard duty is likely to take up its post, not at the nest, but in a nearby sentry tree, where feathers can be preened in peace.

It is of critical importance that the sky-dwelling eagle keep its

7,000 feathers in prime condition. Imperfect ones must be removed. The vanes of those that have become mussed must be straightened. This task is performed with a gently nibbling bill. In particular, flight feathers, which grow on wings and tail, require careful combing. A gland on the bird's rump, when pressed, releases oil that is then applied over the entire body. By rubbing head against breast, the bird is even able to annoint this hard-to-reach place. Upon completing its grooming, an eagle shakes itself to remove any loose feathers it may have missed and to allow its plumage to settle neatly into place. Hours of every day are spent at this essential task.

While the parents are out of sight, the young sleep or watch the sky or may quite suddenly be seized by the need to exercise. As if winding up for take off, one or the other flutters and romps about the nest or flaps its wings continuously for a minute or more. Should a pair of fanning wings be caught by an updraft, they can lift their owner a few feet into the air. And if the wind is high, such a fit of activity may have fatal consequences.

A still flightless nestling that is blown to the ground is doomed. Its parents will answer its distress calls with mournful cries of their own. But impeded by their six- to eight-foot wingspans, they cannot fly into dense vegetation to feed and protect it. If, however, the jettisoned eaglet is sufficiently developed to flop its way to an open area, the adult birds will once again deliver it food. As parents, eagles are impressive creatures.

This is a dangerous time for nestlings. Each day they grow more boisterous. Blood in the shafts of their newly grown quill feathers has not yet dried, a condition that temporarily inflates the birds' size.

This explains why at eleven weeks they are often larger than their parents, with wingspans six inches wider. Their eyrie, which at hatching time seemed enormous, barely contains them. Moreover, it has become flattened by use. The eaglets jump about on it as if it were a trampoline. Now they are able to levitate a few feet into the airspace over their nest, while clutching a stick in their talons. This exercise gives them practice at gripping a perch.

At the sound of a "kek-kek-kek," the parents' alarm cry, however, the eaglets grow quiet. And when a distant whistle alerts them that food is on the way, the giant nestlings hunker down like infants, mantle their wings, and peep. This *begging display* is automatic and must be acted out before the young birds are able to receive food.

One day the older and larger eaglet leaps from its high haven and grabs onto one of the thick branches that support the eyrie. Its landing is clumsy. For several seconds it teeters and beats its wings to regain balance. It cannot yet fly. Over the next week all it can do is hop between nest and tree limb, where it practices the art of branch walking.

The less advanced eaglet can only look on. It is not yet ready to test its perching ability. Now, however, it enjoys an unexpected advantage. For whenever food is delivered, the perching youngster must act out its begging display before it can leap back into the nest. Meanwhile, the nestbound eaglet corners all the food.

But soon it too is out of the eyrie. Now perching and balancing are the important lessons to be learned. The time is fast approaching for each eaglet to launch itself from the nest tree, glide over the forest canopy to a lofty sentry tree and land. And should the young bird fail to grasp the high branch for which it reaches and fall to a lower perch, it could find itself in a poor position to take off again.

Eagles fly like hang-gliders and need plenty of open space and wind flow to obtain lift. So they take care to light on treetops, dead snags or alongside clearings. To be able to pinpoint where it will set down,

a bird must be well coordinated. So perching and balancing are practiced for a week or more before the young eaglets make their maiden flights. Even so, their early touchdowns are wobbly.

The bald eagle does not achieve independence on the day it takes to the air. A bird that is still unable to make a smooth landing is certainly not up to the task of catching a fish. Newly-fledged eagles, in fact, avoid flying over water. Instead they hug shorelines where they feed on carcasses of beached fish. To supplement this diet, their parents continue to bring them meals.

Sometimes food transfers are made on a branch; pieces are passed foot-to-foot from adult to young. More often, however, a sharp-eyed youngster spies one of its parents carrying a bullhead or a northern pike in its talons and heads for the nest, where it makes a great show of begging. Even at this late date, an eagle parent finds this behavior hard to resist. It too flies to the eyrie and donates its catch to the overgrown fledgling.

It is not known exactly when the *immatures*, or fledged eaglets, do learn to fish for themselves. For at least a month after leaving the nest, they frequently return to their former home and dine on food delivered by the adults. During this period, they acquire much skill at flying. And by September they have become the sky dwellers nature intended them to be. On windy days they soar about the heavens playing aerial games. With claws extended, they swoop and roll and dive at one another in mock combat. Sometimes they catch a thermal and ride it higher and higher until they spiral out of sight.

Still they are not able to catch fish and what food they do obtain for themselves is easy pickings. For the most part they *scavenge,* or dine on the remains of creatures they have not killed themselves. With their eagle-eyes they have little difficulty spotting such leavings. Although a partially consumed deer left by wolves or a cougar, a road-killed raccoon or the bodies of storm-battered birds may not sound appetizing to us, to a predator-scavenger like the eagle it is fine fare. Scavengers perform a valuable service. They are nature's sanitation workers, who keep fields and streams and shorelines free of rotting carcasses.

In another month the young no longer need be fed by their parents, and they begin to wander. Unlike truly migratory species, eagles do not follow any particular route, nor do they head for any particular place. Instead they cruise over waterways. In late fall, some scatter to the east; some head west; most, however, wing southward in search of ice-free water to fish in the cold months ahead. Joined by eagles from Canada (birds, of course, do not acknowledge national boundaries), their numbers swell.

48

Winter is a perilous time for inexperienced young eagles. If rivers freeze over or if the birds set down where there is too much competition or if they fall ill or suffer even a minor injury, then capturing a meal may prove impossible. And even a few days of fasting may leave the big birds too weak ever again to hunt. To survive, an eagle must be in top condition at all times.

As if natural hazards were not enough, man has created additional pitfalls for our national bird, ones for which nature has not prepared it. Eagles fly into power lines, get tangled in fishing tackle, sicken on fish taken from polluted rivers, lose their legs in steel-jawed leghold traps, are shot from the sky, are killed for their valuable feathers and die from feeding on the remains of wounded ducks, whose bodies are full of poisonous lead shot.

Few immature eagles make it through their first year of life. Fewer still live to age five when at last they can produce young. Those who do are the wariest of their kind: birds who avoid contact with man. These survivors have also learned how to conserve precious energy and spend long hours of every day just sitting on a branch and loafing. Inactive though they may appear to be, resting eagles are keenly

aware of the world around them. Usually their *loafing perches* over-
look some body of water, so when a sick or injured fish happens to
bob to the surface, the resting bird is in a strategic position to make a
swift attack. In the blink of an eye, it will vanish from its perch,
swoop down and snare itself a meal.

The bald eagle has been criticized by some people for its so-called lazy nature. Even Benjamin Franklin expressed dissatisfaction that such an idler should have been chosen to be our national emblem. In a letter to his daughter, Sarah, he joked that the turkey might have been a better choice. Of the eagle he wrote:

"For my part, I wish the bald eagle had not been chosen as the representative of our country; he is a bird of bad moral character; he does not get his living honestly; you may see him perched on some dead tree, where too lazy to fish for himself, he watches the labor of the fishing hawk [the osprey]; and when that diligent bird has at length taken a fish and is bearing it to his nest for the support of his mate and young ones, the bald eagle pursues him and takes it from him."

Osprey

It is true that bald eagles sometimes rob ospreys of their catch. But it is wrong to apply human values to creatures who must make their way in the wild. Like most predators, an eagle is *opportunistic*, meaning that it takes the easiest meal it can find, whether this be a winter-killed deer or an osprey's hard-won meal. Thus it conserves energy needed for those many occasions when it must pursue and bring down difficult prey. All predators look for windfalls. And a young bald eagle, no less so than an osprey, may be forced to give up its food find to a stronger bird.

Opportunistic feeders not only insure their own survival, their behavior also benefits the prey species upon which they dine. By taking the easiest meal it can find, for example, the bald eagle is bound to remove many dead, sick and weak fish from rivers and lakes. In so doing it helps to stem fish disease and prevents poor specimens from breeding and passing inferior traits to future generations of fish.

Especially in winter eagles need to conserve energy. When temperatures drop the big birds burn food calories just to keep warm and cannot afford to chase after meals they have little chance of catching. At the same time, locating food becomes ever more difficult. As waterways freeze over, they move farther south, exploring tributaries and funneling down major rivers in search of open water to fish. Sometimes they find what they are seeking at a hydroelectric dam, where falling water prevents ice from forming. Here they congregate in large numbers and dine on dying fish, killed by the tailwaters of a power plant. In this case, man's alteration of the natural environment has proved a good thing for eagles.

But eagles need more than food to survive. They are easily disturbed by man's activities and must have privacy. They also need to take refuge from the bitter winds that blow off rivers. In late afternoon, they seek wooded areas and cluster in ancient oaks and sycamores situated behind river bluffs and in sheltered ravines. With feathers puffed out against the frigid air, they look like Christmas ornaments spaced evenly in the leafless branches.

But today eagles have difficulty finding suitable *winter roost sites*. Riverfront property is at a premium and homes and factories and roads and motels now stand where eagles once took shelter. Unless

some tracts of ancient trees can be left uncut, our national bird will not survive.

The big bird's summer habitat is also under siege, as what remains of our great North American forests is cut for lumber. Without suitable nesting areas, eagles will not breed. In fact, conditions must be exactly to their liking before an eagle pair will attempt to rear young.

Still another threat to our national bird is acid rain. A byproduct of industrial smoke, this latest form of pollution is turning our nation's lakes to vinegar and killing millions and millions of fish, the mainstay of the eagle's diet.

Not all the problems we human beings have created for the eagle could have been foreseen. Widespread use of DDT is a good example of misapplied science. For a long time, nobody realized that this chemical, which helped farmers kill insect pests, had gotten into the food chain and was hurting eagles and many other birds as well. The *pesticide* interfered with the birds' ability to make use of an important mineral, calcium. As a result, our national bird began to lay eggs with shells so thin they broke under the weight of the sitting female.

At first no one knew what was causing the problem. In fact, for a very long time, few people realized the bald eagle was even in trouble. One man, however, knew something was terribly wrong and said so.

Charles Broley was a Canadian banker who loved the bald eagle so much that he could hardly wait to retire so he could spend time climbing into nests and fixing bands to the legs of young birds. He was curious to know where the Florida bald eagle population summered; for unlike northern bald eagles, the southern population raises its young in the dead of winter. And in the warm months it takes an out-of-state vacation.

For eighteen years Charles Broley attached identification bands to 1,240 birds, each band reading: "Notify Fish and Wildlife Service, Washington, D.C." In time, some of these bracelets began to be turned in by people who found dead birds. And so Broley eventually collected evidence that many of his Florida birds were summering as far north as Maine, mingling with northern relatives who, at that time of year, were hard at work raising young. The nesting season and migrating timetable of Florida birds and that of northern bald eagles is exactly opposite!

But Broley's work revealed something far more important. In 1946 when he began his fieldwork, he was able to locate and band 150 eaglets. The following year, however, he was not so successful. And every year thereafter he found fewer and fewer chicks in the nests he inspected. By 1955 Broley attached only 8 legbands to young birds in

Florida, even though a few weeks earlier he had seen many more adults sitting on eggs. In 1957, when only 14% of the eggs he counted hatched, Broley knew the eagle was in serious trouble. He connected this hatching failure to mosquito spraying, and he said so. But the United States government paid little heed to Broley's alarming conclusion, for he was not a trained scientist.

A few years later, however, an important book was published which fully backed up Broley's theory. It was written by a woman named Rachel Carson, and it could not be dismissed as unscientific. Rachel Carson not only was a trained scientist, but her book, *Silent Spring*, showed a direct connection between the use of pesticides and the decline of many species of birds. She had chosen her title well. A silent spring was fast approaching, she said, when no birds would be alive to celebrate spring with noisy song.

It would take the government another 10 years to accept the evidence presented in this important book and ban DDT, one of the worst pesticides then in use. Meanwhile, the eagle population continued to decline. Whereas eagles had once raised young in every state except Rhode Island, South Dakota, and Vermont, now only a few states could claim to have any active nests at all.

1973 was an important year for our national bird. Not only was DDT banned in our country, but Congress passed the Endangered Species Act, which granted full protection to America's bald eagle. Since then, what small pockets of breeding pairs have managed to persist have been closely watched by government biologists who climb into their nests and fix bands to their legs and who count their eyries from aircraft. From the information they are gathering, a great deal is being learned about the eagle's habits and its needs.

Today eagle recovery teams are trying out many schemes in an all-out effort to restore the eagle to its former haunts. One technique, called *hacking*, has succeeded in a few places. Young bald eagles are taken from states where the species is now doing well and transplanted to parts of the country where it has become extinct. This is done by hoisting a caged nestling high in a tree or onto a platform, from which it can enjoy a good broad view of the landscape. For several weeks, until the eaglet is ready to fledge, a concealed human being hauls food to it by pulley. The hope is that the surrounding countryside will so *imprint* itself on the young bird that later, when it is old enough to breed, it will return to the area to nest.

Still other people are working to save our national bird at raptor rehabilitation centers, where sick and wounded eagles are brought for treatment. Some victims of bullets, traps, power lines, and poison, can be restored to health. These are set free. Others, those, for example, who have lost a foot in a leghold trap and can never again hunt, are placed in captive breeding programs. What eggs they lay and chicks they hatch are then put into the nests of wild eagles who have not succeeded in producing young of their own. The bald eagle is such an enthusiastic parent that it readily accepts and rears foster chicks.

Many years will pass before it can be known if these efforts to bring back our national bird will succeed. In order for eagle numbers to increase, more birds must be successfully hatched and reared each year than die. And because the bald eagle is, by nature, such a slow breeder, everything possible must be done to encourage it to nest and to retard its death rate. That means nest trees must be protected, birds healed, roost sites purchased, forests spared, the public educated, laws enforced, and the environment cleaned up.

Only then might this stately bird, whose image decorates so many of our nation's coins and buildings and documents, once again grace our nation's heavens. Surely that is the proper place for a sky-dweller to be.

INDEX

J 598.9 R   48840
Ryden, Hope.
America's bald eagle
$11.95

DISCARD

s 5/13 cy 7/01 & circ 10/15